I0165849

SONGS OF FAITH AND HOPE

Meditations on the Psalms

Other Books by Sheri A. Sutton

And So It Is

The Light of Christmas

In Remembrance of Me

Memorable Moments

40 Days, A Journey of Prayer

SONGS OF FAITH AND HOPE

MEDITATIONS ON THE PSALMS

SHERI A. SUTTON

SONGS OF FAITH AND HOPE

MEDITATIONS ON THE PSALMS

© Sheri A. Sutton 2022

ISBN: 978-0-9984548-4-9

Unless otherwise stated, scriptures are taken from THE HOLY BIBLE, NEW INTERNATIONAL VERSION®, NIV®. Copyright © 1973, 1978, 1984, 2011 by Biblica, Inc.® Used by permission. All rights reserved worldwide.

All rights reserved. Without limiting the rights under copyright reserved above, no part of this publication may be reproduced, stored in a retrieval system, or transmitted, in any form or by any means (electronic, mechanical, photocopying, recording, or otherwise), without the prior written permission of the copyright owner of this book.

Sheri A. Sutton
2 Callie Ct.
Wichita Falls, Texas 76310
United States of America
www.sheriasutton.com

ACKNOWLEDGMENTS

With deepest appreciation to Dr. David Hartman for his continued friendship and support as well as his substantive and theological review of this work.

With sincere gratitude to my dear friend and fellow writer, Geneva Rodgers, for her editorial review of this work.

TABLE OF CONTENTS

The Lord is a refuge for the oppressed, a stronghold in times of trouble. Those who know your name trust in you, for you, Lord, have never forsaken those who seek you.

Psalm 9:9-10

INTRODUCTION

We find ourselves today at a time in history where there is division within families and communities throughout the world. Due to our stance on religious beliefs, sexual orientation, gun rights, racism, income disparity, social reform, and a myriad of other issues, our lives become chaotic, stress driven, and, some would say, out of control.

Inundated with technological advances that keep us up-to-date with all that is taking place around us, we are submerged in news feeds, texts, emails, posts, tweets, and blogs that keep us connected every second, minute, and hour of every day. Although technology connects us through information, it can disconnect us from personal contact with those around us which is vital for a healthy lifestyle.

To add to our stress, there are reports across the globe of the casualties of war, random shootings, the Covid pandemic, hunger, loss of jobs, betrayal, abuse, suicide, and many other concerns that wound our spirits and give us feelings of despair and hopelessness. What is the answer to this dilemma of the human condition? Perhaps, we might find a solution in the Book of Psalms.

This treasury of hymns and prayers, written during an extended period of time from approximately 1400 BC to after 538 BC, was called *Sefer* T*ehillim* which in Hebrew means Book of Praises. In English, the word psalm originated from the Greek *psalmos*. These poetic writings were usually accompanied by a stringed instrument and described the ways God was experienced and worshipped.

The Book of Psalms is the longest book in the Bible and is considered theological, doxological, confessional, and practical. The Psalter contains 150 psalms divided into five books. Book I contains psalms 1–41; Book II, 42–72; Book III, 73–89; Book IV, 90–106; and Book V ends the Psalter with psalms 107–150. The earliest psalm of record is number ninety and is the only one attributed to Moses.

The authors of Psalms carefully crafted their writings rich with passion and vivid imagery. The major poetic feature was parallelism—ideas arranged in such a way that balances one element with another of equal importance or similar wording. For Hebrew poetry, this balance of thought was essential and considered more important than sounds or rhythm.

While some psalms speak to God in prayer and about God in praise, others are instructional in form and purpose. Overall, the psalms affirm that God is the center of life and the whole of creation is his one kingdom. Could these ancient writings offer us faith and hope today to soothe our spirits, open our minds, and transform our hearts?

Although used in public worship, the Book of Psalms is also considered by many to be a model for one's devotional life. Filled with intimate and emotional thoughts and prayers, readers may find themselves between the lines and in the words of the psalmist bringing them into a closer and deeper relationship with the God of their understanding.

David, the young shepherd boy who killed the Philistine named Goliath, is attributed with writing approximately seventy-three psalms. According to different translations of the Bible, David is described in 2 Samuel 23:1 as "the hero of Israel's songs, the favorite singer of Israel, the sweet cantor of Israel, and the excellent psalmist of Israel." From the tribe of Judah, David was the youngest son of Jesse and earned the distinction of a great warrior through his many successful war campaigns. He eventually became the second king of ancient Israel uniting all the tribes under his kingship.

But David was not without faults. Stricken by Bathsheba's beauty, an affair began and he instigated the death of her husband, Uriah, in battle. This deception gave way for the marriage of Bathsheba to David. Some of his psalms contain his pleas for mercy and his repentance connected to this transgression. Regardless of his failings, David stayed true to his belief in God and is listed in the genealogy of Jesus.

The psalms of David touch a chord in all of us. In Psalm 6:2–4 he writes, "Have mercy on me, Lord, for I am faint; heal me, Lord, for my bones are in agony. My soul is in deep anguish. How long, Lord, how long? Turn, Lord, and deliver me; save me because of your unfailing love."

Haven't we all been there? Haven't we all been exhausted by the struggles of life? But David, lost, alone, and filled with anguish and despair, cries out for God's saving grace and is confident in God's unfailing love. Perhaps, we should do the same.

In *The Songs of Faith and Hope,* the meditations are inspired by twenty-three Davidic psalms. These psalms contain a message of *hope* found in a *faith* spurred by God's grace and love. According to Hebrews 11:1, faith is "confidence in what we hope for and assurance about what we do not see." Faith gives us hope when we are hopeless and strength when we are weary. In addition, hope empowers us to be the people God calls us to be—people who love instead of hate and who resist the barriers of division thus creating a better world for all.

There are forty meditations included for contemplation. Each one highlights a verse(s) from each of the chosen psalms with some having multiple meditations to consider. To gain the most value from the writings, it is recommended to read each psalm in its entirety. The scripture readings are taken from the Holy Bible, New International Version (NIV). Also, consider writing a personal reflection at the end of each meditation in the space provided.

Although we may not be able to change all outer circumstances of our lives, we can significantly strengthen our inner spirits through prayer and meditation. Hopefully, the devotionals on these particular songs of David will give us the added strength and courage we need during this particular time of our lives.

The Lord is my shepherd, I lack nothing. He makes me lie down in green pastures, he leads me beside quiet waters, he refreshes my soul.

David, considered "the hero of Israel's songs" (2 Samuel 23:1), wrote seventy–three out of the 150 psalms included in the Book of Psalms. As a musician and lyricist, his psalms stand out still today as a profound artistic piece of work. Moreover, David's psalms give us, at least, a glance into his life experiences and, at most, his depth of belief in God's saving grace and unfailing love.

In the verses above, David compares God to a shepherd who gives him what he needs—rest for the body and refreshment for the soul. Don't we all need rest? Our lives often become outrageously chaotic with work, family, activities, and many other items or issues that fight for our time. As we try to manage the messiness of life, our energy slowly slips away, and we are overcome with exhaustion.

David knew that feeling. As a shepherd, he tended his sheep which required more attention and care than other types of livestock. David listened and watched his sheep carefully so that his flock would not suffer undue hardship. The sheep depended on David for food, a safe grazing area, and protection from predators. It was not an easy job and required his attentiveness and commitment.

The sheep knew David's voice and felt his presence as he kept watch. Perhaps they heard David playing a lyre and his voice singing a psalm. And just like the sheep, David listened for the voice of comfort and protection. As the sheep depended on

David, so David depended on God. There was nothing he needed or desired that God would not provide.

In chapter ten of John's gospel, Jesus calls himself the "good shepherd." He cares deeply about each of us. He knows our thoughts before we speak and our voice when we call his name. He knows us to the very core of our being. Don't we have some sense or knowledge about him as well?

In the middle of the night when filled with fear, we hear his still, small voice in our hearts, and we are peaceful. We feel the gentle breeze, the warm sun, or the sprinkles of rain, and we know his touch. We ask for help and experience his power. Through his living transformative presence, we know him. As we navigate this journey of life, it is comforting to know that we can depend on "God with us" to provide all that we need.

CLOSING THOUGHT
John 10:14–15

I am the good shepherd; I know my sheep and my sheep know me—just as the Father knows me and I know the Father—and I lay down my life for the sheep.

PERSONAL REFLECTION

Even though I walk through the darkest valley, I will fear no evil, for you are with me...

David faced many challenges in his lifetime, but one story stands out—the battle with Goliath. Although in the service of Saul as an armor-bearer, David was only a shepherd boy. During this time, the Philistines waged war with the Israelites, and both sides prepared for battle around the Valley of Elah.

Goliath, the famed Philistine giant warrior, urged the Israelites to send someone out to fight. He wagered if he was slain, the Philistines would become the subjects of the Israelites. If not, then the Philistines would have control of the Israelites. David offered to stand against Goliath.

It is not for certain when Psalm 23 was written, but it is hard to imagine a darker valley for a shepherd boy than to fight a giant warrior. Although David had not yet developed his reputation as a great warrior, he was determined to defeat the giant and save his people.

Recorded in 1 Samuel 17:36–37, David said to Saul, "Your servant has killed both the lion and the bear; this uncircumcised Philistine will be like one of them, because he has defied the armies of the living God. The Lord who rescued me from the paw of the lion and the paw of the bear will rescue me from the hand of this Philistine."

Armed with nothing more than a slingshot and five smooth stones, he faced Goliath. Recorded in 1 Samuel 17:50, scripture states, "So David triumphed over the Philistine with a sling and a stone; without a sword in his hand he struck down the Philistine and killed him." With their champion dead, the Philistines retreated. David became known as a great warrior and eventually became the king of Israel.

Psalm 23 speaks to total dependence on God's care and protection. Even in the darkest moments of that day in the valley, David did not fear the circumstances or the outcome. He knew God was with him and would protect him.

We may not be as confident as David when we are faced with the giants in our lives. Still, there is one certainty—God is with us in all circumstances, and his power is beyond any human power. Armed with that assurance, we can go forward regardless of the "giant" in front of us.

CLOSING THOUGHT
Psalm 23:6
Surely your goodness and love will follow me all the days of my life, and I will dwell in the house of the Lord forever.

PERSONAL REFLECTION

I sought the Lord, and he answered me; he delivered me from all my fears. Those who look to him are radiant; their faces are never covered with shame. This poor man called, and the Lord heard him; he saved him out of all his troubles.

One of David's earlier psalms, Psalm 34 has a structure that is quite complex and written in acrostic form. Each verse begins with the successive letters of the Hebrew alphabet. The introduction includes three verses followed by four stanzas developed with verses in sets of four, seven, four, and four. Although complex, it is effective in emphasizing the benefit of faith in God's deliverance. This psalm begins with an introduction of praise for answered prayer and then shifts to wisdom-like instruction.

As recorded in 1 Samuel 18–19, we read that Saul, the first king of Israel, was intimidated by David's many heroic battles against the foes of Israel. He tired of hearing of David's successes and began devising a plan to kill him.

When David became aware of Saul's plans, he went to the Philistine, Achish, king of Gath. Cited in 1 Samuel 21:10–15, David heard comments by the king's servants that made him wary. Fearful of Achish, David pretended to be insane causing the king deep distress. His cunningness allowed him to safely escape, unknown to Achish, to a cave in Adullam, a town southwest of Jerusalem.

It had to be difficult for David constantly running from his enemies, looking over his shoulder, and not knowing what might happen next. However, he did know one thing with certainty—God's faithfulness was steadfast.

In the verses above from Psalm 34, David wrote that when we seek God, he will answer our pleas and deliver us from our fears. Gifted with words and music, David used his talent to commune with God, to meditate on God's presence, and to listen for God's answers. He knew God's help was always available.

There is something transformative that happens when we surrender to a power beyond ourselves. We feel released because we are no longer shackled by the yoke of worry and fear. David must have felt it as he wrote "Those who look to him are radiant, their faces are never covered with shame."

Releasing our struggles to God gives us freedom to focus on the present moment, to enjoy life as we are living it, to love those around us, and to be a light to those stumbling in the dark.

David never failed to acknowledge God's power. He never hesitated to ask for God's help when bound by fear or to admit his worst failures with sincere remorse. Moreover, he never forgot to praise God for his mercy and grace. Perhaps, we can learn to do the same.

CLOSING THOUGHT
Ephesians 5:19b–20
Sing and make music from your heart to the Lord, always giving thanks to God the Father for everything, in the name of our Lord Jesus Christ.

PERSONAL REFLECTION

DAY 4 — PSALM 34:8, 18

Taste and see that the Lord is good; blessed is the one who takes refuge in him...The Lord is close to the brokenhearted and saves those who are crushed in spirit.

David continues in Psalm 34 to reinforce the truth of God's steadfast faithfulness. In verse eight above, he encourages us to "taste and see" the goodness of God. Taste the nectar of a fresh peach or the coolness of fresh spring water. Gaze at the millions of stars lighting the night sky. View the majesty of the mountains, or ponder the depth of the oceans. Hear the music of laughter or a bird's morning song. See the creativity in the all of creation, and ponder its diversity and beauty. It is through our senses that we make discoveries and feel enjoyment. It is, also, through these discoveries that we experience the presence of God.

When was the last time you were brokenhearted? Was a love destroyed, a confidence broken, or a lie revealed? When we lose hope, our hurts become painful and wound our spirits for a long time. How do we begin the journey back to wholeness? Healing begins when we reach out for help. When we are hopeless and surrender our pain to God, freedom begins.

David knew that God was ever present and ready to lift a broken spirit. David was on the run, hiding from those who wanted him dead. But he knew God was with him, empowering him with courage and strengthening his spirit. David never faltered in his faith because he had experienced God's faithfulness, mercy, and grace.

In the beginning of Jesus' ministry as recorded in the gospel of Luke 4:18–19, Jesus went to his hometown of Nazareth. On the Sabbath day, he went to the synagogue and read from the scroll of Isaiah, "The Spirit of the Lord is on me, because he has anointed me to proclaim good news to the poor. He has sent me to proclaim freedom for the prisoners and recovery of sight for the blind, to set the oppressed free, to proclaim the year of the Lord's favor."

Jesus comes to us still today to offer hope, freedom, and joy. His healing power soothes our wounded spirits like a cool balm, releases us from our fears and gives us peace, frees us from the pain of life, and resurrects us from our darkness into the light of God's mercy and grace. That is indeed good news!

CLOSING THOUGHT
Matthew 5:3
Blessed are the poor in spirit, for theirs is the kingdom of heaven.

PERSONAL REFLECTION

I cry aloud to the Lord; I lift up my voice to the Lord for mercy. I pour out before him my complaint; before him I tell my trouble.

It is healing to express our complaints and troubles to someone, perhaps a trusted friend, a family member, or a counselor. It often gives clarity and helps us to see our part in the situation. Often, though, friends and family tire easily of our stories of distress and struggle. So where do we turn? Like David, we can turn to God.

Psalm 142 is one of David's earlier psalms and thought to be another one written when he was hiding in the cave near the town of Adullam. This psalm is shorter than some of his other writings but is still full of his faith and hope in God.

The beginning of this psalm was a cry for God's mercy followed by a pouring out of his complaints and troubles. David had no problem in using the ear of God to relieve the pain and despair he often felt. He was confident in God's healing mercy and his never ending love for mankind.

Writing and music are good ways to ease our pain when going through the difficult times of life. Gathering our thoughts on paper is healing. It enables us to pull the chaos from our minds and see those thoughts in black and white. The writing of prayers and praises help us remember who God is and his importance in our lives.

Music uses our words and melodies to create an art form that touches our hearts and the hearts of those around us. Music is healing. It speaks to us in a universal way and connects us to one another.

David needed relationship. Often hiding and alone, he reached out to God through his psalms as a way to feel connected to something beyond himself. He knew that God was always available, day or night, to listen, to comfort, and to offer peace in the midst of fear and chaos.

We, too, can offer the turmoil of our lives to God and ask for his mercy. We can pour out our complaints, one by one, and know with certainty that he will listen. Then, just like David, we can offer praise for God's compassion and care, and we will experience a gratefulness that fills our heart with joy.

CLOSING THOUGHT
Psalm 142:3
When my spirit grows faint within me, it is you who watch over my way.

PERSONAL REFLECTION

Listen to my cry, for I am in desperate need; rescue me from those who pursue me, for they are too strong for me. Set me free from my prison, that I may praise your name.

One definition of desperate is the utter loss of hope. What, then, is hope? Hope might be defined as trusting with expectancy. It moves us forward, even if we want to stand still and wallow in self–pity. Hope fuels the possibility of healing and transformation.

In the verses above, David wrote, "Set me free from my prison." Prison in this case, theologians believe, was a metaphor for those things that bind us, afflict us, or oppress us. What was David's prison? He was on the run, hunted by his enemies, and separated from his family. Fear and despair was his daily menu, and he felt as if his physical and mental strength was waning.

In desperation, David bet on God's faithfulness and cried out "rescue me." Hope has a way of moving us from despair to action. Hope gives us faith and faith sparks hope. When we have hope, there is a solution to our problems, and that solution is God, who is our sanctuary and shelter from the storms of life.

Refuge is used frequently to define God. For example, consider 2 Samuel 22:3 and 31 "my God is my rock, in whom I take refuge, and he shields all who take refuge in him." Or Nahum 1:7, "The Lord is good, a refuge in times of trouble."

David knew this well. His writings were filled with faith and hope that God would deliver him from his troubles. He was certain that God's power was beyond any human power, including his own. David laid out his problems, admitted his failings, asked for help, and then praised God for his goodness.

God doesn't just do good things, he is good. It is his nature, and it never changes. God comes close to us in times of trouble. He does not stand in the shadows but brings his light into our darkness. When we reach out to God, we open our heart to his heart. We find comfort, relief, and peace. As a result, we are free from those things that fill us with fear and uncertainty. We are free to live in the light of joy and love.

Does that mean that all our troubles will disappear? Probably not. What it does mean, and what David knew without doubt, is that God loves his creation; and because of that love, God is always present and ready to be in relationship with us. His resurrecting power brings us from the depths of dark despair. He heals our hearts, transforms our minds, and strengthens our spirits. God is the only one with that power. Let us take refuge in him.

CLOSING THOUGHT
Psalm 142:5
I cry to you, Lord; I say, "You are my refuge, my portion in the land of the living."

PERSONAL REFLECTION

But I am like an olive tree flourishing in the house of God; I trust in God's unfailing love forever and ever. For what you have done I will always praise you in the presence of your faithful people. And I will hope in your name, for your name is good.

Deceit and betrayal surrounded David's life. He didn't know who to trust because his enemies were everywhere. Trust is defined as to rely on or place confidence in something or someone. When we place our trust in a family member, a friend, or a person of authority, it is devastating when that trust is broken. It takes a long time to recover lost trust, if ever.

After David killed Goliath, King Saul gave David a position in his court on an intermittent basis. During this time, David became an exceptional warrior. After many successes, Saul gave him a high rank in the army, and the troops and other officers were well pleased and appreciated David's achievements. Saul, on the other hand, became resentful, and the seed of jealousy was sown. From that moment, Saul began to plot David's death.

Probably, our life situations are not like David's, and we may not understand his plight. More than likely, however, we have been betrayed, our spirits broken, and our hopes destroyed at some point in time. What can we do in these times of anxiety and distress? David reached out to God.

It must have been difficult for David always running and hiding. He never knew what was waiting around the next bend. Was someone plotting to take his life? Surely, David wondered if he would ever be able to go home again. However, during these times, his psalms tell us that he clung to his relationship with God and knew, without doubt, that he could trust him.

David trusted in God's unfailing love and gained hope through God faithfulness. The verses noted for today's reading begin with a simile, "But I am like an olive tree flourishing in the house of God." Why this comparison?

We know that in ancient Israel olive trees grew abundantly and were crucial for the economy and daily living of the Hebrew people. Olive trees grew well in the rocky soil and the fruit of the trees were not only good to eat but also provided oil for lighting, cooking, and medicinal purposes. According to researchers, the oldest living olive tree in the world is estimated to be 4,000–5,000 years old and is located in Bethlehem.

Perhaps, the olive tree provided an image of longevity and strength for David. Just as God's unfailing love and steadfast promises, David's faith was steadfast and unwavering, much like the olive tree that has lived and produced for centuries.

CLOSING THOUGHT
Acts 12:24
But the word of God continued to spread and flourish.

PERSONAL REFLECTION

DAY 8 — PSALM 56:1-4

Be merciful to me, my God, for my enemies are in hot pursuit; all day long they press their attack. My adversaries pursue me all day long; in their pride many are attacking me. When I am afraid, I put my trust in you. In God, whose word I praise—in God I trust and am not afraid. What can mere mortals do to me?

There are times when we are not so smart. We often claim success for our blessings and believe that we can manipulate people and situations to obtain what we desire. Many times, we proceed without caution and with limited understanding. When we put our trust in our human power, more often than not, we fall short because our power is so limited. But God's power is limitless, and his wisdom is beyond human understanding.

From a shepherd boy to a warrior, David found himself at risk of losing his life. On the battlefield, he knew the circumstances. Off the field, he never knew who might be plotting a threat on his life. He often hid in remote places to stay out of sight from his enemies. Not knowing who to trust or what unexpected circumstance might come his way, David trusted God as his source and deliverer.

No matter what enemies stood before him, he was unafraid. He had confidence that God would answer his cries for help and his enemies would be defeated. David did not doubt because he knew that God was more powerful than any enemy, seen or unseen.

Do we have the faith of David? Perhaps, we can learn from him as we read his psalms and meditate on their meanings. Maybe, we can study David's life more fully and understand his ability to surrender to a power beyond himself. David's gift of writing carried him through many circumstances in his life. It was his way to connect with God through prayer and praise. When he connected with that power, he was empowered to do great things.

Jesus' spent time in the wilderness as recorded in the Gospels. After fasting for forty days and nights, he was alone and hungry. With intent, Satan came to tempt Jesus and cleverly used scripture at times to influence his response. If Jesus was the Son of God, he would turn stones into bread. If he was the Son of God, Jesus would throw himself off the temple's highest point and the angels would save him (Psalm 91:11-12). Then, Satan made one final attempt. If Jesus pledged his allegiance to him, Jesus would have all the kingdoms of the world. However, Jesus had fortified himself while in the desert by his constant contact with God through prayer and meditation. For every attempt that Satan made to draw Jesus away from his purpose, he was thwarted by God's power through Holy Scripture.

The study of scripture is vital to our faith development. Satan used it to reinforce his lies. Jesus, on the other hand, used scripture to shine God's light on those lies to reveal the truth. Just like Jesus and David, God will strengthen us through his Word when we face the temptations of life.

CLOSING THOUGHT
Philippians 4:13
I can do all this through him who gives me strength.

PERSONAL REFLECTION

DAY 9 – PSALM 56:12–13

I am under vows to you, my God; I will present my thank offerings to you. For you have delivered me from death and my feet from stumbling, that I may walk before God in the light of life.

By definition, a vow is a solemn promise, a pledge, or an oath. It is also defined as a declaration of something that one will do. According to the Book of Psalms, David made several oaths to God. In Psalm 7:17, David vowed to give thanks to God and sing praises to his name. In Psalm 66:14, he pledged to fulfill his vows to God when he was in trouble. In today's reading, David was adamant about his vows to God. Not only did he write that he was under *vows* to God (emphasis inserted), he continued by declaring his praise to God through offerings of thanksgiving.

Why did he write so deliberately about his vows to God? For David, God recognized all his grievances and sorrows. He delivered him from physical death, but he also delivered him from a spiritual death. David's constant connection to God through prayer and writing nurtured his relationship with God and also strengthened his assurance of God's faithfulness.

Throughout scripture, God proclaims his promises to humanity. "I will never leave you nor forsake you" (Joshua 1:5). "For God so loved the world that he gave his one and only Son, that whoever believes in him shall not perish but have eternal life" (John 3:16). "And surely I am with you always, to the very end of the age" (Matthew 28:20). God never breaks his vows to us, but we are not so faithful.

Man has a tendency to break or delay his promises. There is always an excuse followed by another vow to do it differently. A marriage vow for a life–long commitment ends in divorce. A signed contract agreement is broken without reason or notice. We promise God that we will live with integrity, love, and respect. Then, we fall short and make excuses.

God offers us much more—life, love, peace, and hope. God creates us and breathes into us the breath of life. He loves us extravagantly, a love that covers us with his mercy and grace over and over again. He gives us peace that comes from within even when the world is filled with chaos. And God gives us hope—hope for a better future and for a peaceful world—a world where God's love is clearly evident in the words and actions of all mankind. God offers us what no one can, and it is his vow to us.

CLOSING THOUGHT
Jeremiah 29:11
"For I know the plans I have for you," declares the Lord, "plans to prosper you and not to harm you, plans to give you hope and a future."

PERSONAL REFLECTION

But you, Sovereign Lord, help me for your name's sake; out of the goodness of your love, deliver me. For I am poor and needy, and my heart is wounded within me. I fade away like an evening shadow; I am shaken off like a locust. My knees give way from fasting; my body is thin and gaunt. I am an object of scorn to my accusers; when they see me, they shake their heads.

Psalm 109 is another song with an intricate composition. David begins with his petition to God, "My God, whom I praise, do not remain silent" (v. 1). He continues with verses describing the injustices of his enemies against him, and follows with the listing of requested punishment for the offenders as well as the aspects of their ruthless character.

Then comes the turn in the psalm—David writes the verses noted above for today's meditation. It is interesting that he compares his plight to the fading of an evening shadow. Shadow is used in various scriptures throughout the Bible with usually one of two meanings—either as protection (e.g. the shadow of God's wings) or signifying something that is not fully revealed (e.g. the kingdom of heaven).

However, David seems to be using this simile to represent a kind of death. Just as evening shadows disappear as the sun sets, so can the light of life fade as we are overwhelmed by the struggle of fear and despair.

In one moment, life's struggles can take us from the heights of ecstasy to the depths of the abyss. Betrayal and deceit by those we love feel like the earth is opening up beneath us, and all we can do is fall into the darkness.

David, however, knows that all is not lost because the psalm again petitions for God's help. Even though David is weighed down with his struggles, he also has faith in God's power and unfailing love.

Psalm 109 ends with David praising God for his salvation, not on his merit but on God's unfailing mercy. There is a joy expressed in these last lines as David professes that God stands "at the right hand of the needy" (v. 31) and is always ready to appear on their behalf against the foes of life. We, too, can be assured that God is ready to help and protect us. Just like David, all we need to do is ask and believe God's faithful promises.

CLOSING THOUGHT

Do thy friends despise, forsake thee? Take it to the Lord in prayer!
In his arms he'll take and shield thee; thou wilt find a solace there.

Hymn – What a Friend We Have in Jesus
Lyrics by Joseph Scriven, 1855
Music by Charles Converse, 1868

PERSONAL REFLECTION

I call on you, my God, for you will answer me; turn your ear to me and hear my prayer...Keep me as the apple of your eye; hide me in the shadow of your wings from the wicked who are out to destroy me, from my mortal enemies who surround me.

Psalm 17 is one of David's prayers and may have been written during the tenth century BC. It begins with a petition in verse one, "Hear me, Lord, my plea is just; listen to my cry." Again, David reaches out to God in prayer when he is under attack by his enemies.

In today's scripture, David called on God with assurance that God would not only hear him but also answer him. He did not ask for God's help prompted by his situation but based on a daily relationship with God. That relationship brought confidence that God would listen to David's requests.

In addition, David asked in verse eight to "keep me as the apple of your eye." This phrase designated something or someone who was loved above all others. David knew that God loved him, and, with assurance, he then made another appeal, "hide me in the shadow of your wings."

This phrase is a traditional Hebrew metaphor against oppression and also speaks to the image of shade that protects from the hot desert sun. We might, also, imagine a bird sheltering her young to brood and protect them. There is safety under the wing of the mother, and there is safe refuge under the wing of God.

David's psalms tell us over and over again how much God loves us extravagantly. He is ever present in our lives. He is faithful to his promises and offers us hope in the midst of our darkest hours. However, to believe as David is not an easy task for most of us.

It is difficult to surrender to a power beyond ourselves, to let go of our preconceived expectations, and to be rigorously honest with ourselves, let alone God. Often we become fearful that we will not get what we want or lose what we have. Consequently, we become paralyzed which prohibits us from moving forward.

God's story however, as presented in Scripture, reveals to us time and time again that his power, understanding, and vision is so much more than ours. As we read and study the Psalms, perhaps we too can open our hearts to the mystery of God and find the comforting peace that strengthened and sustained David throughout his life.

CLOSING THOUGHT
Psalm 17:15
As for me, I will be vindicated and will see your face; when I awake, I will be satisfied with seeing your likeness.

PERSONAL REFLECTION

DAY 12 – PSALM 63:1

𝄞 *You, God, are my God, earnestly I seek you; I thirst for you, my whole being longs for you, in a dry and parched land where there is no water.*

David was a master poet, and his imagery added depth to his story of redemption and faith. As recorded in 1 Samuel 24–26, David was hiding in the desert of En Gedi, which is located along the western shore of the Dead Sea. In the beginning of this psalm, David wrote of his yearning for God like his thirsting for water "in a dry and parched land."

Suppose we were in a desert with no water in sight. Our bodies would yearn for a cool, satisfying drink of water. We would frantically search for traces of water because our lives would depend on it. It would be unbearable when our life energy would begin to drain. For David, he felt that pain in his yearning for God.

David longed for the presence of God just as our bodies crave a refreshing drink of water. He sought God earnestly for he knew God's power and strength were the answer to his dilemma. Without God, his spirit would surely wither and die.

We learn in chapter four of the Gospel of John that Jesus was traveling to Galilee and had to pass through Samaria. He was hot, tired, and thirsty. He sat down by Jacob's well to rest under the hot noon sun. A woman approached the well to draw water. Jesus asked for a drink. Because there was hostility between the Jews and Samaritans, she was perplexed by his request. Then Jesus began to tell her of the living water he offered that would forever satisfy her thirst

Water is necessary for life, and often we thirst from a lack of water. But Jesus was pointing out to the Samaritan woman that we can also thirst from spiritual need—the longing for God when we are lost in the deserts of life. Often, we try to quench that "thirst" with worldly substitutes that leave us empty and unfulfilled. Jesus, however, offers mankind living water, "a spring of water welling up to eternal life" (John 4:14) that fills our being and makes us whole.

Like David, we yearn and thirst for God, the aching deep within our spirit that nothing in this world can satisfy. Only God's living water conquers our thirst and allows us to flourish even in the droughts of life.

CLOSING THOUGHT
John 4:10
Jesus answered her, "If you knew the gift of God and who it is that asks you for a drink, you would have asked him and he would have given you living water."

PERSONAL REFLECTION

DAY 13 – PSALM 63:2–3

I have seen you in the sanctuary and beheld your power and your glory. Because your love is better than life, my lips will glorify you.

While hiding in the desert, David had opportunities to use his power for personal gain or in service to God. In the final two confrontations between Saul and David, the tables were turned. Saul was at the mercy of David.

Power is intoxicating and can be used for the good of mankind or for personal fame and fortune. In the Sermon on the Mount, Jesus speaks to this dilemma. "So when you give to the needy, do not announce it with trumpets, as the hypocrites do in the synagogues and on the streets, to be honored by others" (Matthew 6:2).

We all want recognition for the good things we do in the response to the needs of others or for the things we do to better ourselves. Some use this recognition to build their self–esteem and to stand out among their peers. True self–worth and acknowledgment, however, come from one's relationship with God.

The term sanctuary used in today's scripture may be defined as a consecrated place, a place for worship, or a place of refuge and protection. Sanctuary can also mean our inner place of peace and calm, perhaps achieved through meditative practices. Then, there is God's sanctuary—wherever we experience him.

David had experienced God in all areas of his life—on the battlefield, hiding in a cave or in the desert, and in relationships with friends and enemies. He knew God's power and his faithfulness, and he trusted him. God was his sanctuary, his safe place, and his place of peace.

When we become overwhelmed with life, when we are running from the results of our choices, and when we have lost it all with nowhere to turn, we can turn to God. From the deepest part of our spirit, we can offer it all to him, and we can find peace. It is a peace that we cannot explain. It is "the peace of God, which transcends all understanding" (Philippians 4:7), and it is the peace that fills us completely. Surely, in that moment, our lips will glorify God.

CLOSING THOUGHT
Psalm 63:6–8
On my bed I remember you; I think of you through the watches of the night. Because you are my help, I sing in the shadow of your wings. I cling to you; your right hand upholds me.

PERSONAL REFLECTION

I will praise you, Lord, among the nations; I will sing of you among the peoples. For great is your love, higher than the heavens; your faithfulness reaches to the skies. Be exalted, O God, above the heavens; let your glory be over all the earth.

Psalm 108 is a combination of verses from two other psalms of David's, Psalm 57:7–11 and Psalm 60:5–12. The message of Psalm 108 is one of assurance, a song of praise and hope for God's love and faithfulness as well as continued victory over David's enemies.

According to David, God's love stretched over all of creation, farther than the heavens, and surpassed all other love. Because of this extravagant love, David wanted to exalt the glory of God over all the earth.

Imagine the depth of God's love for each of us. There is no other love of that magnitude. We may think that our love for our spouse, our children, or our grandchildren is that encompassing. Many times, however, our love is conditional. Although, we may want to love someone without strings attached, are we capable of loving as God loves us?

Love also requires faithfulness which moves us to consider the qualities of commitment, consistency, and loyalty. Are we committed in our relationships? Are we loyal to those we love? Are we consistent in our words and actions? Those traits are challenging to practice on a daily basis. Love is, to say the least, difficult.

David knew first hand of God's love and faithfulness. He knew of God's mercy and grace that was extended to him in spite of his shortcomings. David knew well this love that transcends worldly love, and he desired that others would know the expanse of God's love too. Through David's words of prayer and praise, he spread the message of God's power and love.

In Scripture, we learn that God is "slow to anger, abounding in love and forgiving sin and rebellion" (Numbers 14:18). Like David, we can experience today this same intimate relationship with God assured of his love and faithfulness. Our stories can also reveal God's redemptive power that brings us out of the darkness of our lives into the light of his love. Then, we will sing words of praise and thanksgiving from our joy-filled hearts to God's listening ear.

CLOSING THOUGHT
Psalm 108:1–2
My heart, O God, is steadfast; I will sing and make music with all my soul. Awake, harp and lyre! I will awaken the dawn.

PERSONAL REFLECTION

Give us aid against the enemy, for human help is worthless. With God we will gain the victory, and he will trample down our enemies.

According to 2 Samuel 8:6b, "The Lord gave David victory wherever he went." At times, when alone and isolated, David had doubts. Nevertheless, he always gave God credit for the blessings of his life. David was resolved in his praise of God, and nothing ever interfered with his reverent awe of the mercy and grace given to him.

In today's scripture, David was adamant that human help was worthless, but with God victory was assured. During this time, David had many successes on the battlefield. He was a skilled warrior and led his men well. But David knew that human power, without God's power, was ineffective and led to disastrous outcomes.

Why is it so difficult to admit that we need help to navigate life? Why do we waste our time and effort in battles we cannot win alone? Human nature is puzzling.

Many times, we base the important decisions in our lives on our prideful self–will instead of God's will. It is easier to manipulate situations than to wait on God's direction. However, our decisions often result in unguided maneuvers that can lead us down a path of unhappiness away from the character traits of integrity, faithfulness, and truth. Although, it may be easier to follow the ways of the world than the ways of God, we can compromise ourselves and lose our integrity.

David relied on God's power because he had experienced it over and over again. God's abundant faithfulness and his overflowing portion of mercy and grace never ceased to amaze David. Throughout his life, he continually lifted his voice in song to praise the one whom he trusted and loved.

Life is a series of choices, and our choices result in a series of consequences. We can choose to go into battle alone, or we can benefit from David's example. One leads us toward defeat because we are unarmed and unprepared. The other leads us to victory with God leading the way.

Closing Thought
Deuteronomy 20:4
For the Lord your God is the one who goes with you to fight for you against your enemies to give you victory.

Personal Reflection

In my distress I called to the Lord; I cried to my God for help...He reached down from on high and took hold of me; he drew me out of deep waters. He rescued me from my powerful enemy, from my foes, who were too strong for me.

Psalm 18 gives us an artistic recount of God's saving help in answer to prayer. This song of deliverance is another cleverly crafted psalm. It begins with an introduction in verses one through three. The body of the psalm is divided into three major divisions: God's deliverance in verses four through nineteen, the moral grounds for God's help in verses twenty through twenty–nine, and God's assistance detailed in verses thirty through forty–five. The psalm concludes with verses forty–six through fifty.

Although there are some minor variations, this psalm is also found in 2 Samuel 22. According to the title notes of Psalm 18, this writing is based on the time that God delivered David not only from all of his enemies but also from the hand of Saul. This is significant, for as the psalm suggests, God's actions cause David's life to flourish: "You, Lord, keep my lamp burning; my God turns my darkness into light" (v. 28).

Found in the very first verse of the psalm, David immediately sets the tone for the entire work, "I love you, Lord, my strength." He praises God for the strength that has helped him conquer his enemies. There is no doubt whose power has sustained David when reading these opening verses.

How do we describe our enemies? Maybe over extended debt is a problem, perhaps a divorce causes pain, or possibly our position at work is eliminated. Maybe, we wait for the results of a medical test. We feel the earth trembling under our feet. Fear permeates our spirit, and we lie on the battlefield gasping for breath.

David, in the midst of battle, called out to God for help. He was confident that God would come to his aid, and the course of his life changed. His enemies, at that moment in time, were conquered, and David was saved.

How does David's experience speak to us today? God's help is ever present and available when we are surrounded by those persons or situations that harm us. As we pray for the reality of God to be manifested in our lives, transformation begins. Solutions to our problems become clearer, our thoughts and actions change, and our broken spirit heals.

This transformation may not happen suddenly. However, like David, over time we will know without doubt that God is our refuge and our deliverer from the struggles and trials of life.

CLOSING THOUGHT
Psalm 18:2
The Lord is my rock, my fortress and my deliverer; my God is my rock, in whom I take refuge, my shield and the horn of my salvation, my stronghold.

PERSONAL REFLECTION

It is God who arms me with strength and keeps my way secure. He makes my feet like the feet of a deer; he causes me to stand on the heights.

In the scripture above, David continues his psalm of praise for God's deliverance. For most of us, we may not immediately praise God for lessening our burdens, providing us peace, or delivering us from our enemies. Most likely, we continue our everyday lives as if we solved all our problems on our own initiative and power. In addition, we may look at the world and wonder if "God with us" is still true today.

In the Book of Habakkuk, a dialogue between God and the prophet is recorded. Many questions filled Habakkuk's mind as he struggled to comprehend God's intentions in the world when there was so much wickedness. For Habakkuk, God's timing and solutions were difficult to understand. Then, one day, he watched a deer cautiously find its way along a treacherous cliff. Suddenly, he realized that whatever might come his way God would surely guide him through the perilous times of life just as he guided the deer. Habakkuk finally grasped that God was his strength. Even if all was lost, God still existed and was ever ready to guide and protect.

Just like the prophet, we may struggle for answers to the ways of God. However, faith is born as we search and struggle to understand. It is our tool for accepting God on God's terms. Although we may never fully understand, we can rest in assurance that God is working toward the greater good of all mankind.

Like David, we can know about God's faithfulness and love first hand through our relationship with him. As a result, we may find that God is always present and equips us with truth, righteousness, and peace. In addition, he fortifies us with faith, salvation, and his word. God's armor gives us strength and resolve to walk through whatever the circumstances of life. Then we may realize that David's writings ring true for us as well. God's ways are perfect, his word is flawless, and his refuge is truly a place of safety.

CLOSING THOUGHT
Psalm 18:35
You make your saving help my shield, and your right hand sustains me; your help has made me great.

PERSONAL REFLECTION

DAY 18 – PSALM 4:1, 8

Answer me when I call to you, my righteous God. Give me relief from my distress; have mercy on me and hear my prayer...In peace I will lie down and sleep, for you alone, Lord, make me dwell in safety.

Although Psalm 4 is a short writing, it is to the point. With a sense of urgency, David asks for God to answer his prayers and give him relief from his distress. If God answers, then David will experience peace.

How many of us have decisions to make or need answers to questions? We live in a world where time speeds by us with no regard to our needs or wants. Often, we don't take time to thoughtfully consider our decisions because time is money. We are on the fast track to nowhere; and, yet, we want God to answer us now!

Waiting is one of the hardest parts of life, especially, if we're waiting on God's intervention. Even though David begins this psalm with a demand, he does so with the expectancy that God will answer. He uses the word righteous to define God. By some scholars, the righteousness of God is parallel to his faithfulness. Others define his righteousness as one of his divine attributes. God always acts in consistency with his own character.

As we have seen in the psalms of David, he believed in God's faithfulness and love. He had been here before imploring God to save him from his enemies, from those who slandered him, and from those who wanted him dead. Regardless of the circumstance, David always praised God for his protection, intervention, and rescue.

When we read through David's psalms, it is apparent that he found peace in God's safety and refuge. In other psalms, this peace is referred to as "a spacious place." If we consider this description, what comes to mind? Perhaps, it is a place with room to move around, or a place with harmony instead of conflict. Maybe, it is a place with no worries or struggles, just a deep sense of serenity.

This place of peace is not found outside ourselves. It is found within. When we connect with God through prayer on a daily basis, something extraordinary happens. Our attitudes, perceptions, and responses change. We are no longer bound by the power of the world but released by God's resurrecting power.

David was a master of meaningful prayer written from the depths of his spirit. He cried out to God, confessed to God, and sang praises to God. Still today, his prayers are a model for all of us. When we go to God in prayer, hiding nothing but releasing all, transformation begins. And through that transformation, we will lie down and sleep.

CLOSING THOUGHT
Job 11:18
You will be secure, because there is hope; you will look about you and take your rest in safety.

PERSONAL REFLECTION

DAY 19 – PSALM 27:5

♩ *For in the day of trouble he will keep me safe in his dwelling; he will hide me in the shelter of his sacred tent and set me high upon a rock.*

Fear is a yoke around our neck that holds us hostage. By definition, fear is caused by being alarmed by a perceived danger or threat. It can cause worry, panic, and anxiety. Fear can also paralyze us to such an extent that the feeling of powerlessness overcomes us.

David knew about fear. His enemies were always hiding in the shadows and war called him to battle time and time again. In Psalm 27, David wrote a triumphant prayer about deliverance. Even in the midst of trouble and the pain of betrayal, David was confidently assured of God's safety and refuge.

Various verses of this psalm can be traced back to 2 Samuel as well as 1 and 2 Chronicles. According to some scholars, this psalm was written after David's victory over foreign enemies, including the Philistines and the Moabites, as recorded in 2 Samuel 8. In addition, it was most likely written before David's affair with Bathsheba and the manipulated death of Uriah.

David writes of God's sacred tent being his shelter. In various places in the Bible, God's tent is also referred to as his sanctuary, hiding place, shadow, or presence. If we consider all of these terms, we may gain more understanding as to what David was describing.

A tent is a waterproof outdoor shelter that protects and gives a place to rest. A sanctuary is a place for religious worship. But, in this psalm, the more likely definition is a place of refuge and protection. A hiding place is self-explanatory and does give the image of a safe haven for hiding from one's enemies or, per-

41

haps, the struggles of life. The shadow from a tree, for example, provides shade from the hot, blistery sun. Finally, presence gives a totally different image in that it implies shelter and protection simply by being in the company of God.

Based on these images, it is apparent that there is safety and refuge wherever we experience God. When we commune with God on a daily basis, our spirit is strengthened so that we become spiritually fit to face the struggles of life.

David also writes of God setting us high upon a rock. A rock of substantial size is secure and immovable and can be a strong foundation for building. If God is the foundation of our lives, then we are prepared for whatever trials of life come our way. Our hope in God's faithful deliverance gives us strength so that we can move forward unafraid.

CLOSING THOUGHT
Psalm 27:1
The Lord is my light and my salvation—whom shall I fear? The Lord is the stronghold of my life—of whom shall I be afraid?

PERSONAL REFLECTION

DAY 20 – PSALM 27:13-14

I remain confident of this: I will see the goodness of the Lord in the land of the living. Wait for the Lord; be strong and take heart and wait for the Lord.

David ended Psalm 27 with a concluding note of confidence. He was certain that he would see the promises of God's covenant in his life. Do we declare that same confidence in our lives?

It is difficult to recognize God working in the world today. Many experience injustice and war. Others struggle daily to provide the necessities for their families. Health issues loom over some people as well as the high cost of living. We see chaos in the streets and children unsafe in their classrooms. One side believes their views are better than the other side. However, we see no compromise or solutions to the many problems we all face today.

How did David believe so assuredly that he would see God's goodness while he lived? Sometimes we have to shift our focus and look beyond what we see at first glance. If we open our eyes, there is always a story of healing, heroism, renewal, and victory.

Someone diagnosed with cancer beats the odds and lives with a new outlook on life. Emergency responders save a home from being burned down or rescue a drowning child. Another person is offered a new position with a higher income and can now cover the monthly outgo of expenses. People of varying backgrounds come together to establish a neighborhood watch program so that they can live in a safe environment. If we consciously look at the world around us, we will find the stories of victory and deliverance.

David also reminds us to wait. Most of us don't like to wait because we want answers now. We want to see God's presence in the world now, and we want our dreams to come true now. Waiting seems unbearable. We can't see God working in the background to bring about the greater good. We, certainly, can't fully understand the workings of God or his timing. His understanding is far beyond ours, and he has his own timeline.

So, perhaps, we need to be more like David—remain confident, be strong, and wait for God. Often, we fail to realize that in those times of waiting extraordinary things can happen. So, we wait expectantly—wait for God to teach us, protect us, and ready us for the experiences of our lives.

CLOSING THOUGHT
Isaiah 30:18
Yet the Lord longs to be gracious to you; therefore he will rise up to show you compassion. For the Lord is a God of justice. Blessed are all who wait for him.

PERSONAL REFLECTION

Have mercy on me, O God, according to your unfailing love; according to your great compassion blot out my transgressions. Wash away all my iniquity and cleanse me from my sin.

Psalm 51 is another intricate song written with a two-line opening that balances the two-line closing. In between, four stanzas comprise the body of the song. This psalm is a plea for God's forgiveness for the wrong David committed.

There was no doubt that Bathsheba was beautiful. When David saw her that night on the palace roof, he could not resist temptation. David's affair was complicated. Even though Bathsheba was married, David wanted her at any cost. He even arranged for her husband's death in battle. What drove him to make that decision of betrayal? Was it the seduction of power? Was it the thrill of the forbidden fruit? Or was it a moment when David simply did not listen for God's guidance but chose, instead, to follow his own desires?

It's an age-old story. We are tempted and forget everything we have known about living a godly life. We all have had those moments when we all fall short of God's glory. Temptation stares us in the face, and we succumb to the fantasy playing in our head. Most of the time, those experiences do not end well. Hearts are broken, people are hurt, and lives are destroyed.

Because David knew he had committed a transgression against God, he humbled himself and asked for forgiveness. Like David, when we have a truly sorrowful and repentant heart, we can admit our failings and humbly ask God for his mercy. He will hear our cries and forgive us. Forgiveness is God's gift of grace. Even when we think it's impossible, his grace pours over us like flood waters.

All of us will make decisions that hurt others; and, ulti-mately, regret those choices. However, we have hope that is built on the faith of God's resurrecting power. It is a power that can pull us out of the darkness of our unhealthy choices and bring us into the light of his compassion, mercy, and unfailing love. We don't have to live in the shadow of our shame. We can recreate our lives built on God's foundation of redeeming grace and live lives based on honesty, integrity, and truth.

CLOSING THOUGHT
Psalm 51:10–12

Create in me a pure heart, O God, and renew a steadfast spirit within me. Do not cast me from your presence or take your Holy Spirit from me. Restore to me the joy of your salvation and grant me a willing spirit, to sustain me.

PERSONAL REFLECTION

DAY 22 – PSALM 32:5

♪ *Then I acknowledged my sin to you and did not cover up my iniquity. I said, "I will confess my transgressions to the Lord." And you forgave the guilt of my sin.*

In Psalm 32, David once again wrote about the consequences of sin, the freedom found in confession, and the acceptance of God's grace.

The unhealthy choices we make can prey on us for a long time and cause a spiritual sickness exacerbated by guilt and shame. According to David, there is a solution. Lay your failures before God with a humble and repentant heart. It may sound easy, but it is not.

Our pride is the culprit. It keeps us from admitting our faults to ourselves or to anyone else. We even hesitate to admit our faults to God, even though he already knows them. For some reason, it is difficult to humble ourselves. The consequence, then, is to carry the guilt and shame of our transgressions with us until we are suffering from overwhelming fatigue, a life threatening disease, or the hardening of our spirit. We die a little more every day until we are a shell of the person God created.

David writes of this dilemma in verses three and four, "When I kept silent, my bones wasted away through my groaning all day long. For day and night your hand was heavy on me; my strength was sapped as in the heat of summer." Suffering in silence is not a healthy choice. Even if we are embarrassed by our actions, the alternative of not facing our faults is bleak.

David experienced time and time again God's saving grace. He knew that God's power to forgive and love was immeasurable and steadfast. David's faith and hope in God's redemp-

47

tion moved him to do the things that were the most difficult to do.

When Jesus, God Incarnate, came to love us up close and personal, he did the unfathomable. He gave himself for humanity's sin. He sacrificed himself on a cross so that we all might be loosed from the chains of this world into the freedom of God's eternal kingdom.

It is difficult to imagine the scope of God's love for his creation and even more difficult to accept it. We would rather carry the burdens of our shortcomings with us every day than to admit them and ask his forgiveness.

The good news is that God expectantly waits for us to seek his mercy and grace. When, finally, we cry out to him in desperation, his love delivers us from the heaviness of our failures. Then we can sing about God's faithfulness and the hope found in his infinite redemptive love.

CLOSING THOUGHT
Psalm 32:7
You are my hiding place; you will protect me from trouble and surround me with songs of deliverance.

PERSONAL REFLECTION

For the word of the Lord is right and true; he is faithful in all he does. The Lord loves righteousness and justice; the earth is full of his unfailing love.

What is truth? It is defined in part as a fact, the fidelity to a standard, or a spiritual reality. We expect the truth when we ask for answers to our questions, when someone confesses their love, or when our leaders address the problems of the world. But, in today's volatile climate, our expectations of the truth fall short.

Look around—the world is in chaos. Turn on the television or read a newsfeed. It is difficult to believe what we see and hear. Most of the time, it is someone's opinion which may or may not be the truth. Each political party has their own version of the state of the nation. Corporations make decisions based on the bottom line, and everything changes by the next news segment. Marriage vows are taken, then, fidelity is broken. We each have our own interpretation of our life, sometimes true and sometimes imagined or embellished. Many profess to live godly lives, but their words and actions don't support their claim. So where do we find the truth, the real truth, and nothing but the truth?

According to David, the word of God is the truth because he is faithful and unchanging. God is the same as yesterday, today, tomorrow, and forever. He doesn't shift because of the popular belief of the week. He loves his creation too much to lie or be unfaithful. It is not in his character to do anything that would compromise his promises to us

Scripture tells us over and over again of God's faithfulness and his unfailing love. It assures us of his fidelity. It gives us the spiritual reality of Jesus to show us the depths of God's re-

49

deeming power and love. Because of these promises, God assures us a life full of his mercy and grace.

When God made us in his image, it stands to reason that he gave us his character traits. As we build a relationship with God through prayer, those traits are made known to us. It is our responsibility to make them our own so that in everything we do and in every word we speak we will be known as people of truth.

Living a life built on God's principles is not easy in the world today where there is division, distrust, and disrespect. However, if we believe in God's truth and live by his truth, we will experience the deep joy of his love and the freedom of his peace. And that is reason to sing a new song!

CLOSING THOUGHT
Psalm 33:2–3

Praise the Lord with the harp; make music to him on the ten-stringed lyre. Sing to him a new song; play skillfully, and shout for joy.

PERSONAL REFLECTION

DAY 24 – PSALM 33:9, 11

For he spoke, and it came to be; he commanded, and it stood firm...But the plans of the Lord stand firm forever, the purposes of his heart through all generations.

In Genesis 1and 2, we read the stories of creation. From the formless and empty darkness, God called into being light, the sky, the waters, and dry ground. He separated day and night and commanded the land to produce. He let creatures swim, birds fly, and animals live on the land. He breathed life into mankind. Then, God saw that all he had made was very good. God's word was creative; and when he spoke, his word was powerful and steadfast.

We might look at God's creation today and shake our heads. The beauty of creation seems lost on a world that spins too fast and works too hard. Do we ever take time to stop and imagine the world being created? What would the world look like today if there were no wars, no hunger, no separation, and no fear?

In the middle of all of life, there is God. Even as we look at the world and wonder if we are doomed, God is present. In his presence, we find hope—hope for peaceful resolutions, for changes in circumstances, and for reconciliation. The hope found in God's love for mankind gives us peace in our spirits. It gives us courage to ask the difficult questions, and it moves us beyond our suffering.

According to David, the plans of God are firm forever. What are the plans of God for each of us? Perhaps, we are to glorify God in all that we do. Living our lives as a reflection of God's glory certainly would change the world. Maybe, as Jesus taught, we are to love our neighbor as ourselves. To love without judgment and expectations would definitely affect change in the world.

If God's plans depend on us, are we willing to participate? Are we ready to look at ourselves honestly and change our behaviors? Are we prepared to give even a little of our resources to help others? Are we eager to suit up and show up for what God calls us to do? These are difficult questions that each of us must answer.

David had certainly done unacceptable things in God's eyes. Still, he was used in the redemptive plan for the world. David hoped in God's faithfulness and unfailing love because he knew God's promises were assured for all generations.

Closing Thought
John 17:20–21

I pray also for those who will believe in me through their message, that all of them may be one, Father, just as you are in me and I am in you. May they also be in us so that the world may believe that you have sent me.

Personal Reflection

From heaven the Lord looks down and sees all mankind; from his dwelling place he watches all who live on earth—he who forms the hearts of all, who considers everything they do.

It is comforting to know that God watches us. Because he loves us, he sees us through the eyes of love. However, does it sadden him to hear all the words we say or see the actions we take? According to David's psalm, God considers everything we do.

It may be difficult for us to believe that God cares about us even when we don't live up to his vision and desires for us. Maybe, that is our experience as a parent. Many times, what we envision for our children is not how their lives evolve. As parents, we don't always know what's best nor have all the answers, but we usually have a dream for our children's future. However, life happens and those dreams may never come to fruition. Regardless, we don't stop loving and caring about them.

God loves and cares about us even when we go astray. In the Gospels, we find the story of the shepherd who takes care of his sheep. He keeps them safe and knows their name. When even one sheep is lost, the shepherd goes to find the one while leaving the others behind. There is not one sheep that is not important to him. Likewise, there is not one person in all of mankind that is not important to God.

David's experience as a shepherd surely strengthened his understanding of God's love and faithfulness. Even when David fell short of God's teachings and principles, God's love never wavered.

David not only knew of God's unfailing love but also knew the power of his deliverance. He considered in Psalm

33:16-19 that no king was saved by the size of his army or his own strength, nor could a strong horse in battle save his rider. Regardless of man's strength or tools used, he could not win without God's power. David always, without fail, put his hope in God's love and power to redeem and deliver him.

At times, we may think that God has abandoned us. There are times when we must wait for his answers to our questions or relief from our struggles. We can be assured, however, that God is always moving in us and around us to bring forth his purpose in our lives. Just like David, we can move forward with the anticipation that God considers all that we hope for and imagine.

CLOSING THOUGHT
Psalm 33:20–22
We wait in hope for the Lord; he is our help and our shield. In him our hearts rejoice for we trust in his holy name. May your unfailing love be with us, Lord, even as we put our hope in you.

PERSONAL REFLECTION

Yes, my soul, find rest in God; my hope comes from him. Truly he is my rock and my salvation; he is my fortress, I will not be shaken. My salvation and my honor depend on God; he is my mighty rock, my refuge. Trust in him at all times, you people; pour out your hearts to him, for God is our refuge.

In this psalm, David offsets it with a two-line opening and a two-line closing. In between are three parts; and the second part, verses five through eight, is a thematic hinge. Verses five and six echo the opening verses while verses seven and eight anticipate the closing verses. David's composition, although intricate in form, is a simple expression of trust.

In addition, the psalm title included "for Jeduthun," who was a Levite and one of three choir leaders. He was also responsible for the sounding of the trumpets and cymbals. In addition, it was Jeduthun's task to play the other instruments for sacred songs.

When David wrote this song, he knew the perils of war and being hunted by his enemies. He was constantly on guard, whether on the battlefield or hiding in a cave. He had to be ready at any moment to defend himself. He had little rest, and his body was weak most of the time.

We can relate. The war is not always between nations or about political unrest. Sometimes, daily life is the battle. We clash with family members, we compete with co-workers for the promotion, we struggle to provide for our families, and we battle to stay safe from a health pandemic. The battlefield is bloody and the wounded are many. How do we escape from the insanity of it all?

David expressed his trust in God with the image of a fortress. A fortress was a stronghold, an area of safety, and a place of protection. Many times it was built on the side or top of a mountain. Often, it was constructed with water separating it from the mainland. However, the psalmist was not speaking of a literal fortress. He was speaking about God.

God is our true fortress. He is our rock of stability, our protector in times of trouble, and our deliverer from the perils of life. Through daily prayer and meditation, we come to know the character of God. We begin to trust in his power, faithfulness, and love. Then, we know with certainty the truth. It is in him that we find rest. It is in him that we find salvation, and it is with him that we win the battles of life.

CLOSING THOUGHT
Psalm 62:1–2
Truly my soul finds rest in God; my salvation comes from him. Truly he is my rock and my salvation; he is my fortress, I will never be shaken.

PERSONAL REFLECTION

DAY 27 – PSALM 55:12-14

If an enemy were insulting me, I could endure it; if a foe were rising against me, I could hide. But it is you, a man like myself, my companion, my close friend, with whom I once enjoyed sweet fellowship at the house of God, as we walked about among the worshipers.

David wrote Psalm 55 as a prayer for God's aid in the sorrow of betrayal by someone he loved. Some theologians identified Ahithophel as the enemy written about in this psalm. Ahithophel was one of the king's counselors involved with the conspiracy led by Absalom, the king's son.

It is devastating to be betrayed by someone you trust. It tugs at your heart and fills your mind with doubts and unanswerable questions. Betrayal is, at best, a confidence shared unknowingly. At its worst, it is a traitorous violation of trust. And when it is a friend or a family member, the pain is agonizing and long-lived.

Jesus knew the pain of betrayal. One of his disciples, Judas, handed him to the authorities for thirty pieces of silver. Jesus was charged, found guilty, and died on a cross. When Judas came to his senses and was filled with remorse about the wrong he committed, he hanged himself. One way or the other, the deadliness of betrayal affects everyone involved.

David was overcome with grief and hurt, and so he turned to the one who could comfort him. He turned to God and poured out his hurt and grief. David always turned to God almost immediately because he knew that God would give him courage for battle and rescue from his enemies. Moreover, he knew that God would heal the hurt in his heart.

David had a process for dealing with the situations of life. He began with a plea to God, "Listen to my prayer" (v. 1). Then, the request was followed by his reason, "My heart is in anguish" (v. 4). In detail, he explained the situation as listed in the verses for today's reading. Finally, his psalm ended in praise for God's unfailing love and deliverance, "Cast your cares on the Lord and he will sustain you" (v. 22).

At times, we are so caught in the tornado of despair and fear that we forget to ask God for our rescue. God loves us, sustains us, and protects us. Yet, we struggle and obsess until we are weary and empty. Eventually, we reach out to that power beyond ourselves that can and will help us. Why is mankind so determined to live by his own power and understanding? Sometimes we are so afraid of the unknown that we hesitate to surrender to God—the one who can do more than we could ever imagine.

In the midst of his fears, David implored God to do what he couldn't—save David from himself. And when he had finished praying, he gave praises to God. Perhaps, we should do the same.

CLOSING THOUGHT
Psalm 55:1–2
Listen to my prayer, O God, do not ignore my plea; hear me and answer me.

PERSONAL REFLECTION

As for me, I call to God, and the Lord saves me. Evening, morning and noon I cry out in distress, and he hears my voice. He rescues me unharmed from the battle waged against me, even though many oppose me. God, who is enthroned from of old, who does not change...

Psalm 55 continues with David's answer to his dilemma, God. In the verses above, David writes descriptions of God that warrant our attention. He saves, hears our voices, rescues, and does not change.

God saves, comes after "I call to God." A personal name holds power. It identifies, gives recognition, and distinguishes one from another. As soon as we speak God's name, he hears us. When we identify the majesty of God, we can let go and let him resurrect us from the power of our problems. With surrender, we finally know freedom and peace.

The last description that David gives is that God does not change. From the beginning of time, God has watched over his creation. He has been the presence in our spirits calling us to be in relationship with him. He has lighted our paths and walked with us through the joys and sorrows of our lives. He has been, and continues to be, the foundation of our faith and the giver of extravagant love and abundant grace.

It is comforting to know that in a world shifting and changing around us moment by moment, God is the same as he was yesterday, as he is today, and as he will be tomorrow. When everything else in life seems uncertain and limited, God is limitless, beyond the stars and the seas. He is ever present, moving in us, through us, and around us.

David knew God's power, love, and grace. He testified about it over and over again and claimed God to be true and steadfast. Regardless of David's failures and shortcomings, he never doubted that God loved him and protected him.

We, too, can have the faith of David. We can be sure of God's never ending love and steadfast faithfulness. We have proof over and over again in Scripture that God is ever ready and available to conquer our fears, heal our spirits, and restore us to wholeness. He continually walks with us and intercedes for us when we are hopeless, in despair, and full of fear. When we cry out for help, he hears us and responds. In this moment and every moment, God is with us.

CLOSING THOUGHT
Psalm 55:22
Cast your cares on the Lord and he will sustain you; he will never let the righteous be shaken.

PERSONAL REFLECTION

When I called, you answered me; you greatly emboldened me....your love, Lord, endures forever—do not abandon the works of your hands.

Defined as a state of thankfulness, gratitude is prevalent in most of David's psalms. Psalm 138 is much less intricate than many of David's writings. The message, however, rings loud and clear—it's a song of praise and thanksgiving for God's deliverance.

Living a joyful life depends on an attitude of gratitude as touted by many who have lived a long and fruitful life. It has also been said that there is a gift in every circumstance if we are willing to see it. Those statements may be difficult for some.

Many worry every day if there will be food to eat or water to drink. Some live in fear of job loss or home foreclosure. Even those of us who don't have those worries may have some equally distressing ones—the loss of a loved one, a life-threatening illness, or the safety of our children. Our problems are relative to our situations, and our troubles are no more or less important than our neighbor's.

When we are in times of struggle and fear, those situations may give us clarity as to our own behavior, may lead us to understand someone else's personality or problems, or may propel us to love more freely and live more courageously. It has been said that we live life forward but understand it in hindsight. Usually, we do not have understanding in front of the struggles of life. It is only after we have lived through our difficult situations do we gain any understanding or wisdom at all.

David was full of gratitude for God's abiding love and his abundant grace. He was quick to give God credit for all the good things in his life and swift to ask forgiveness for his failings. Even on the battlefield and surrounded by enemies, David's confidence in God's faithfulness spurred him to seek communion with God on a daily basis and to ask for help without fear. As a result, David felt gratitude and filled his songs with thanksgiving.

God's steadfast faithfulness and merciful love greatly empowered David to do what was needed and to stay devoted to God's teachings. As a result, he felt gratitude and continued to praise and glorify God with all his heart. Imagine what the world would be if we all adopted an attitude of gratitude!

CLOSING THOUGHT
Psalm 138:5
May they sing of the ways of the Lord, for the glory of the Lord is great.

PERSONAL REFLECTION

DAY 30 – PSALM 30:11–12

You turned my wailing into dancing; you removed my sackcloth and clothed me with joy, that my heart may sing your praises and not be silent. Lord my God, I will praise you forever.

All of us mourn at different times in life and for different reasons. Mourning can be silent, as in holding our feelings deep inside, or it can be released in loud wailing. The Israelites often wore sackcloth, coarsely woven goat hair made into a garment, for times of mourning. David was mourning according to this psalm.

Life can be difficult. At least, for David, life was often painful to bear. Sometimes, his behavior prompted his difficulties, and other times those who hated and despised him made his life miserable. In this particular psalm, David was on the brink of death. Was he physically ill? Or was he depressed headed toward the abyss of spiritual hopelessness?

It happens to all of us. Life throws us an unexpected curve in the road, and we are not prepared. Have we've been diagnosed with an illness? Are we on the precipice of financial ruin? Do we grieve the end of a career or the loss of a loved one? Tragedies come in different shapes and sizes catching us off guard and filling us with doubt and despair. What do we do?

David called out to God. He had pleaded with God before for help and deliverance. In this psalm, however, David wrote that God turned his wailing into dancing, his mourning into joy.

How does God do that? How does he take us from the depths of despair into his light of mercy and grace? His resurrecting power is the key. If God can resurrect Jesus from the tomb of death, shouldn't we expect that he can bring us out of our darkness? Shouldn't we believe that God's power is more than strong enough to alleviate our difficulties?

David believed in God's power and strength because he had experienced it over and over again. God never failed to give David the help he needed and never withheld his love, mercy, grace.

For some of us, it can be difficult to accept that God would want to help us with our problems—God won't help me, not after all the things I've said and done. Contrary to our thinking, the reality is that God loves us extravagantly and especially wants us to find joy and freedom in our lives.

It is not always easy to travel the road in front of us. Sometimes, it is scary and foreboding. At times, it is difficult to maneuver the obstacles in our way. But when we call out to God for help, he hears us and responds. Then, we can remember God's promise, "Never will I leave you; never will I forsake you" (Hebrews 13:5), and we will sing loudly with great joy.

CLOSING THOUGHT
Psalm 30:2–3

Lord my God, I called to you for help, and you healed me. You, Lord, brought me up from the realm of the dead; you spared me from going down to the pit.

PERSONAL REFLECTION

You have searched me, Lord, and you know me. You know when I sit and when I rise; you perceive my thoughts from afar. You discern my going out and my lying down; you are familiar with all my ways. Before a word is on my tongue you, Lord, know it completely.

The final collection of David's psalms, 138–145, is included in Book V of the Psalter. Of these eight writings of David, Psalm139 is a wonderful poetic piece about the greatness and goodness of God.

It is comprised of four sections, with each section containing six verses. The theme of searching and knowing begin and conclude the psalm. Overall, this psalm is a prayer for God to examine the total being of the psalmist, focusing on God's relationship with the individual. David opens with the affirmation that God knows him perfectly and completely.

Parents know their children, even before they are born. They sense the fragility, innocence, and movement of the unborn child. Parents visualize their babies still in the womb and call them by name. They begin to love. When the baby is born, they deliberately search his face, count her fingers and toes, smell her skin, and hold him close to imprint upon their hearts this new and precious child. Out of a crowd of hundreds of babies, parents instinctively know their child.

And so it is with God. He created each of us, with intent and purpose, and thoroughly knows our hearts, minds, and spirits. He recognizes each from the other and identifies us in the lineup of life. When we are lost, God finds us. When we despair, he comes to us. When we are troubled, he offers us peace. When we question, he gives us answers. God is familiar with all our ways in every area of our lives. He misses nothing and sees it all. He knows each of us to the depth of our being and, yes, still loves us.

And isn't that the good news? Someone, who knows us so completely, still loves us so passionately. He looks beyond our shortcomings and sees his creation. He never forsakes us, and his love never waivers. He looks beyond our faults and sees his child, fragile and delicate, a miracle waiting for love. With assured confidence, we can know that we are always under the watchful eye and loving hand of God.

CLOSING THOUGHT
Psalm 139:23–24

Search me, God, and know my heart; test me and know my anxious thoughts. See if there is any offensive way in me, and lead me in the way everlasting.

PERSONAL REFLECTION

DAY 32 – PSALM 139:7-8

Where can I go from your Spirit? Where can I flee from your presence? If I go up to the heavens, you are there; if I make my bed in the depths, you are there.

In the verses above, David stated that no matter where he was, God was there. He continued in verses nine through twelve that God was in the heavens and the depths; "the wings of the dawn and the far side of the sea"; and in the darkness of night and the light of day.

There is nowhere that we can go where God is not already there. We can't hide from him, and we can't escape. Be assured, God is wherever we are, even in times of darkness.

There are times in life when we are rejected, alone, and miserable. We want the pain to go away, but we also want to wallow in our misery. Yet, everywhere we look, there is God. We see his beauty in the morning sunrise and experience his majesty in the glittering night sky. We see his love on the faces of friends and family. He is there, and we can't avoid him. Nothing can obscure his presence except our own obstinate self–will. If we stop the insanity of separation and breathe in his comfort, peace, and grace, we may find that his love shelters us and offers us safety.

Isn't that the irony of humanness? We resist God, yet he is the one who will comfort us the most. Sometimes in our resistance, we discover that we have nowhere else to go. God is beside us, in front of us, and behind us. He is everywhere.

Paul had experienced the presence of God. He knew that God was with him in times of personal struggle as well as in times of persecution. During his entire ministry, Paul's faith in God sustained and strengthened him. In response, he wrote in Romans 8:38–39, "For I am convinced that neither death nor life, neither angels nor demons, neither the present nor the future, nor any powers, neither height nor depth, nor anything else in all creation, will be able to separate us from the love of God that is in Christ Jesus our Lord." Paul, like David, knew that "God with us" filled him with hope and strengthened his faith.

We can know the same. Wherever we go and whatever our circumstances, we can be assured that God is present in every moment for all time.

CLOSING THOUGHT
Exodus 33:14
The Lord replied, "My Presence will go with you, and I will give you rest."

PERSONAL REFLECTION

My frame was not hidden from you when I was made in the secret place, when I was woven together in the depths of the earth. Your eyes saw my unformed body; all the days ordained for me were written in your book before one of them came to be.

David continues this psalm by affirming that God knew him intimately through his creation. In Genesis 2:7, we read that "God formed a man from the dust of the ground and breathed into his nostrils the breath of life, and the man became a living being."

God created the world and all therein with intention. Each of us was created, not as an afterthought, but for a purpose. Furthermore, when God created, he saw that it was good.

However, life takes us down many paths with twists and turns, and sometimes we make unhealthy choices that are detrimental to our wellbeing. The psalm ends with David asking God once again to search his heart, to bring to light any offensive faults, and to lead him by God's principles and values. That is a courageous request but is necessary in order to live a godly life.

It takes courage to lay our heart, mind, and spirit before God for his inspection. But it takes even more mettle to listen to God's reply and apply his guidance. Most of us look for the easier, softer way. After all, rules have loopholes, and God gives us free will to make our own choices. That is true. But if we are to live a life of devoted holiness, we must be fearless in our pursuit and take action to rid ourselves of self–defeating behaviors.

It is easy to see the shortcomings of others. However, it is very difficult to see our own character flaws. A life of integrity requires an ongoing rigorous examination in the ways that we fall short of God's glory. Daily, we can make the decision to be vigilant in our quest to be the person God created us to be. Most likely, we still will make errors in judgment and possibly unhealthy choices, but we can continue to progress toward the worthy goal of an authentic life.

David knew God's unfailing love and steadfast faithfulness. He knew his intimate, ongoing relationship with God gave him hope. If he fell short in his quest for a holy life, he knew with certainty that God would be there to hear his confessions, to love and redeem him, and to move him forward day by day in his pursuit of a holy life.

Like David, when we surrender our will and life to God, he will search our hearts and shed light on our character traits that are detrimental to us. Then, he will lead us gently into the way everlasting.

CLOSING THOUGHT
Psalm 139:13–14

For you created my inmost being; you knit me together in my mother's womb. I praise you because I am fearfully and wonderfully made; your works are wonderful, I know that full well.

PERSONAL REFLECTION

I waited patiently for the Lord; he turned to me and heard my cry. He lifted me out of the slimy pit, out of the mud and mire; he set my feet on a rock and gave me a firm place to stand. He put a new song in my mouth, a hymn of praise to our God. Many will see and fear the Lord and put their trust in him.

The whole of Book I of the Psalter is framed by Psalms 1 and 2 and Psalms 40 and 41. These four psalms are declarations of blessedness that result from making healthy choices: Psalm 1:1, "Blessed is the one who does not walk in step with the wicked"; Psalm 2:12, "Blessed are all who take refuge in him"; Psalm 40:4, "Blessed is the one who trusts the Lord"; and Psalm 41:1, "Blessed are those who have regard for the weak."

Psalm 40 begins with David recounting his past experiences with God. He knows firsthand of God's power, mercy, and grace. Therefore, David has a new song of praise laced with hope for a better future.

Verses six through ten constitutes the structural center of the psalm, "I desire to do your will, my God; your law is within my heart" (v. 8). This verse reminds us that there is a struggle within all of us between our desire to follow God's will or to follow the will of the world.

It is not easy to walk the path that God sets before us. There are many obstacles along the way: money, success, and prestige to mention a few. Even with our best intentions, our desires for achievement and acceptance can tempt the best of us and lead us down a path of unhappiness. Paul writes in Romans 7:15, "I do not understand what I do. For what I want to do I do not do, but what I hate I do." That is the dilemma for all of us.

David knew that God loved him regardless of his circumstances or faults. He also knew that God would liberate him from the yoke of his weaknesses and strengthen him through his struggles. His faith in God was unwavering.

God knows our faults and the desires of our hearts as well, and we can trust, just like David, in his unfailing love for each of us. If we listen closely, we may hear him whisper his desire for us—a life of significance filled with deep joy and true freedom.

CLOSING THOUGHT
Proverbs 3:5–6
Trust in the Lord with all your heart and lean not on your own understanding; in all your ways submit to him, and he will make your paths straight.

PERSONAL REFLECTION

DAY 35 — PSALM 40:11-12

Do not withhold your mercy from me, Lord; may your love and faithfulness always protect me. For troubles without number surround me; my sins have overtaken me, and I cannot see. They are more than the hairs of my head, and my heart fails within me.

David continued Psalm 40 with a prayer. He asked for God's mercy, protection, and deliverance. He wrote about the magnitude of his faults and failures that had overtaken his life. Then, David requested that God consider his circumstances and help him. He ended his prayer with simple assurance: "You are my help and my deliverer, you are my God, do not delay."

If we need financial assistance, we often go to an advisor or a banker. If our car is in need of repair, we seek a reputable mechanic. Or if we have a health issue, we make an appointment with a medical specialist. We take these steps so that we can receive the best advice or assistance needed. It would be undesirable to do anything less.

However, how quickly do we turn to God when we are knee deep in the struggles of life? Are we so arrogant to believe that we can solve all of our problems and trials through our own power? There is a power available to all of us that can eliminate the fear and chaos of our lives. Yet, we tend to ignore it until life spins out of control and there are no other options. Our free will is our dilemma.

Our humanness stands in the way of a joyful and peace-filled life. More often than not, we continue in our struggles with the idea that we have all the answers and, at some point in time, we will solve our problems. Yet, the truth of the matter is that we don't have all the answers. Whatever we think we know, we probably don't.

David knew that God held the answers to his everyday struggles. Because God's power was beyond any other power available to him, he also knew that God was his refuge, his place of safety.

We may not have the same problems as David—leading an army into war or being hunted by his enemies. But our struggles are just as daunting. If we remember that God's resurrecting power overcame the power of death, wouldn't it be to our advantage to tap into that power for the problems in our lives?

Surrendering our problems and concerns to God may be difficult. We may fear that we will not get what we desire or lose what we hold dear. However, when we let go of our expectations and wait for God to work in our lives, we will gain peace of mind, faith in a power beyond ourselves, and hope of a better tomorrow. Then we will know what David knew—"Blessed is the one who trusts in the Lord" (v. 4).

CLOSING THOUGHT
Psalm 40:17
But as for me, I am poor and needy; may the Lord think of me. You are my help and my deliverer, you are my God, do not delay.

PERSONAL REFLECTION

🎼 *Hear me, Lord, and answer me, for I am poor and needy. Guard my life, for I am faithful to you; save your servant who trusts in you. You are my God; have mercy on me, Lord, for I call to you all day long. Bring joy to your servant, Lord, for I put my trust in you.*

Psalm 86 is one of the last six psalms in Book III of the Psalter and is the only one in that book attributed to David. We find a carefully crafted poem comprised of five stanzas with the verse counts of four, three, three, three, and four. Verses eight through ten serve as the center of David's prayer and includes his fundamental belief in verse nine—God's sovereign and universal rule. God's righteousness, love, and faithfulness are the key concepts of this psalm much like other Davidic writings.

In this prayer, David requested God's deliverance from the struggle of enemy threats—those outside and his weakness within—and began by stating in verse one that he was poor and needy. This resonates with the first Beatitude found in Matthew 5:3, "Blessed are the poor in spirit, for theirs is the kingdom of heaven."

We may think of poor in spirit as meaning those persons who are downtrodden, ostracized by society, or unhappy due to various reasons. Could it be that Jesus intended a deeper meaning? Many believe that they can live their life fully void of a power beyond themselves and live day by day based on their own standards and power. Some may have success and happiness that way, but many only find disappointment, resentment, and unfulfilled dreams.

However, when we realize that our power is limited and our arrogance of self–sufficiency is detrimental to a fruitful life, we have two choices—to continue on our own or to surrender to a power greater than ourselves. In that moment, we are "poor in spirit" because we are acknowledging the foolishness of our thinking. As we begin this process of surrender, God's begins his transformation within us.

David knew that his life was being dramatically changed day by day by God's mercy and grace. With certainty, he knew that God was faithful and his love eternal. Consequently, David never hesitated to praise God for being present in his life.

We can also be assured of God's existence in our lives. When we reach out in prayer, God hears us and answers. He comforts us when we mourn, fills us with his love when we are alone, and surrounds us with his grace when we fall short. When we offer praise for his presence in our lives, he hears us and gives us abundant joy. Perhaps, that joy is the essence of the kingdom of heaven.

CLOSING THOUGHT
Romans 15:13
May the God of hope fill you with all joy and peace as you trust in him, so that you may overflow with hope by the power of the Holy Spirit.

PERSONAL REFLECTION

Day 37 – Psalm 86:11, 13

Teach me your way, Lord, that I may rely on your faithfulness; give me an undivided heart, that I may fear your name...For great is your love toward me; you have delivered me from the depths, from the realm of the dead.

David continues Psalm 86 by asking God for an undivided heart. We know that undivided means whole or not separated into parts. Another definition is focus, as in undivided attention.

When David requested an undivided heart, he seemed to be asking for a heart that only focused on God as the source and ruler of his life. Following his request, he wrote "that I may fear your name." In this context, fear probably meant respect or to regard as holy. Why did David include this request in his prayer and what might this mean for us today?

In Matthew 6:24, Jesus stated, "No one can serve two masters. Either you will hate the one and love the other, or you will be devoted to the one and despise the other." David wanted his focus to be entirely on the sovereign God, the Creator of the world and all therein.

In life, we often are pulled in different directions. With relationships, home, and work, our time is divided between where to be and what to do. For example, many get distracted from a healthy home life while making money to support the family. Money becomes the object of success, and the family suffers by being set aside. The focus is diverted from a more important part of life to another aspect of life. Although financial security is a prudent endeavor, this alternate focus becomes the force that drives our lives and may continue to weaken our family units.

How can we keep our focus on what matters most? First, we determine what guides our lives. If we believe that living a godly life is of utmost importance, then secondly, a relationship with God is our primary purpose. That relationship, consequently, deserves attention on a continuing basis to guide and direct the entirety of our lives. To develop that relationship, we take a third action to dedicate time every day in study, prayer, and meditation. This commitment to our relationship with God will broaden our understanding of who he is to us and who we are to him.

If we spend time in developing a relationship with our Creator, then the other aspects of life will fall in place. Our home will be more peaceful, our relationships more loving, and our work experiences less stressful.

When we come to know God on a deeper level, we recognize and honor his holiness. As a result, we come to realize the divine within ourselves. With that understanding, we will become aware of the divine in all of God's creation and sing with voices of praise, "For you are great and do marvelous deeds; you alone are God" (v. 10).

CLOSING THOUGHT
Psalm 86:12
I will praise you, Lord my God, with all my heart; I will glorify your name forever.

PERSONAL REFLECTION

DAY 38 – PSALM 145:3, 9

Great is the Lord and most worthy of praise; his greatness no one can fathom...The Lord is good to all; he has compassion on all he has made.

Included in Book V of the Psalter, Psalm 145 is a song of praise and another thoughtfully composed work of David. This hymn to God is written in an acrostic poetic form using the twenty-two letters of the Hebrew alphabet as the initial letters for the sequence of verses.

Between the two-line opening (vv. 1–2) and the closing verse (v. 21), there are four stanzas highlighting the attributes of God—greatness, goodness, trustworthiness, and righteousness. The first two stanzas (verses 3–7 and 9–13a) are each five lines with the remaining two stanzas (verse 13b–16 and 17–20) having four lines each. In addition, line eight, hidden between lines seven and nine, is another significant theme, "The Lord is gracious and compassionate, slow to anger and rich in love" and echoes Exodus 34:6–7, when God proclaimed his name and renewed his covenant with Moses.

David was indeed a master poet and able to express his faith and hope in God by a skillfully crafted artistic form. In the verse for today, David began by claiming that the greatness of God was unfathomable. In other words, David could not, and we cannot today, comprehend the majesty of God. He's beyond definition and his works cannot be catalogued according to present day classifications.

Thirty-seven chapters into the Book of Job, God finally speaks in 38:2, "Who is this that obscures my plans with *words without knowledge*" (emphasis added)? The response of all responses! Many times we try to describe God with words that fall short. Can we really explain the majesty of God? What words describe God's glorious greatness or extraordinary goodness? How do we explain the workings of God? It is beyond our imagination and our ability to express.

God is beyond time and space. His understanding is not our understanding. Consequently, his purpose and plan for the whole of creation is too magnificent for us to even begin to understand, much less explain. How then do we communicate the greatness and goodness in our lives as the result of our faith and hope placed in this one true God?

Like David, we tell our story to the best of our ability of how God works in our lives and how his power transforms us day by day. Every day, we live in faith that God will reveal himself to us in ways that we least expect. As we continue to live our lives, we are hopeful for the day that the veil will be lifted and we will see more clearly the majesty and grace of God.

CLOSING THOUGHT
Psalm 145:4
One generation commends your works to another; they tell of your mighty acts.

PERSONAL REFLECTION

DAY 39 – PSALM 145:13

Your kingdom is an everlasting kingdom, and your dominion endures through all generations. The Lord is trustworthy in all he promises and faithful in all he does.

David continues Psalm 145 by expressing the everlasting presence and trustworthiness of God. Everlasting means never-ending, endless, or eternal. Imagine for a moment the endlessness of God. What comes to mind—the enormity of space or the depth of the seas? David writes that God's sovereignty endures through all generations. How many generations have known and believed in the eternal God? Too many to count.

David also wants us to recognize that God is trustworthy and faithful. If we look at some of the promises of God, perhaps we can discover what David means. "The Lord will fight for you" (Exodus 14:14). "So do not fear, for I am with you" (Isaiah 41:10). "I will give you rest" (Matthew 11:28). "I have overcome the world" (John 16:33).

God is concerned with each individual, and, at the same time, he is the Supreme Being over all of creation. God is indeed a mystery, and we cannot fully understand his love, power, or grace. However, we can know with certainty that God is honorable and good.

Human beings are disappointing. We make promises to appease those around us, then break them. We swear an oath to be ethical and honest, then neglect to honor our word in business dealings. We make marriage vows to last a lifetime then fail to respect those vows through the difficult times.

Even when we make promises to God to live a righteous life, to be compassionate to others, to be inclusive, and to take care of the people and the world around us, we fail miserably.

We don't have a good track record for being trustworthy or faithful. Thankfully, God does.

We can trust in God's promises because he is who he says he is, and he does what he says he will do. He cannot be or do anything differently. He is the one true God, faithful and trustworthy. He is the same in this moment as he is in all moments for all time.

CLOSING THOUGHT
Revelation 21:5
He who was seated on the throne said, "I am making everything new!" Then he said, "Write this down, for these words are trustworthy and true."

PERSONAL REFLECTION

DAY 40 – PSALM 145:17-18

The Lord is righteous in all his ways and faithful in all he does. The Lord is near to all who call on him, to all who call on him in truth.

David ends Psalm 145 with the righteousness of God. Righteousness is defined as morally right or genuine. We think of someone who is righteous as following God's principles to live a godly life. Why did David choose to end his composition with this aspect of God?

This particular psalm's structure builds on the aspects of God's character. Ending with righteousness reinforces the other aspects that David includes. God can only be great, good, and trustworthy because he is morally right and genuine. This righteousness is the basis for who God is and is the catalyst for the other qualities that David lists.

What does this mean for us today? Perhaps, we should examine in depth our own character, beginning with the word genuine that is defined as authentic or true. If we want to live an authentic life, we must face the truth about our character. Looking at ourselves without blinders takes courage. When we observe what we say versus what we do, it can be painful, especially if we fall short of who we think we are. However, seeing our true selves is enlightening. Only when we truly know ourselves can we begin to make the necessary changes to live an honorable life.

Change is difficult. Old behaviors can be like our most comfortable pair of shoes. Even when they are worn out and falling apart, we don't want to let go because we wear them every day. They are a part of us. Our character traits are the same. We resist changing our behavior because it feels comfortable and we receive some benefit from it. However, in the end, that old behavior becomes unhealthy and detrimental to our spirit.

The good news is that God is faithful and stands ready to walk with us through this process. With our sincere commitment to change, he grants us courage to tackle this daunting task so that we can move toward wholeness.

When we strive to be who God created us to be, we realize that our story of faith and hope based on God's genuine promises can help those struggling around us. When we help to strengthen the community of faith, God is more visible to a world that needs his love and grace. Then, we will sing praises to his holy name forever and ever.

CLOSING THOUGHT
Hebrews 10:23
Let us hold unswervingly to the hope we profess, for he who promised is faithful.

PERSONAL REFLECTION

AFTERWORD

As we have discovered through the meditations offered in this book, David had an authentic relationship with God. He bared his soul before him, laying out his transgressions and his pleas for help. And God heard him and answered.

There are many things we can learn from spending time meditating on the psalms of David. The obvious is his masterful craft of writing. It is apparent that David had a gift with words, but also with the art of structure. Every psalm is skillfully laid out with precision and purpose. The psalms included in *Songs of Faith and Hope* are rich in poetic devises such as imagery, simile, and metaphor. In addition, David's use of repetition intensifies his message found within.

There is another aspect of these psalms that is central to their impact for us today. They are passionate, vivid, and real. In many of his writings, David leads us through a sequence of petitions for help, repentance for his failures, and finally his praise for God's redemptive power and faithfulness.

This raw honesty reveals the complete authentic intimacy of David's conversations with the Creator. This interaction, though, is only found through the expression of genuine listening and responding. When we can open our whole person to the presence of God—not only the joy of life but also the failures and disappointments, the sorrow and the pain—and listen for his guidance, transformation begins in that moment.

Although David had many faults, as we all do, his relations with God never faltered. He never turned away, even when he was full of despair and emptiness. He continued to thank God for all his blessings, to praise God for his faithfulness, and to live with the hope found in God's redeeming love.

And shouldn't we do the same? Like David, we can have that intimate relationship with the Creator and know that he is at work in our lives guiding us with his merciful love, showing us his continued faithfulness, and redeeming our lives every moment of every day. When we come to realize the genuine active presence of God in our lives, just as he was always present in David's life, we too will sing a new song of praise and thanksgiving! And when our song is heard, the world will once again have "confidence in what we hope for and assurance about what we do not see" (Hebrews 11:1).

But I trust in your unfailing love; my heart rejoices in your salvation. I will sing the Lord's praise, for he has been good to me.

Psalm 13:5-6

ABOUT THE AUTHOR

Sheri A. Sutton is an author, devotional writer, and poet. Her newest book, *Songs of Faith and Hope,* is a collection of forty meditations focusing on the power of the Psalms. In addition, her devotional writing has been published in the *Secret Place* devotional magazine and the *Lenten Devotions on the Lord's Prayer.* Sutton also has been published in the following Advent e-devotional publications *Calm and Bright, Chrismons,* and *He Is Called.*

As a member of the Wichita Falls Poetry Society and the Poetry Society of Texas, Sutton has been recognized in various local and state contests. Her poetry has been published in her work, *Memorable Moments,* as well as the *Wichita Falls Literature and Art Review* magazine, The Poetry Society of Texas' *A Book of the Year, Lifting the Sky, The Secret Place,* and the *2023 Texas Poetry Calendar.*

For a limited time, she wrote a monthly newspaper column while serving on the Community Editorial Board of the Times Record News.

Sutton also offers professional services that include writing and editing for books, newsletters, and other materials for individuals, companies, or organizations. Visit her website, www.sheriasutton.com, for more information.

Sutton and her husband, Lloyd Mark Sutton, live in Wichita Falls, Texas.

www.ingramcontent.com/pod-product-compliance
Lightning Source LLC
La Vergne TN
LVHW041201080426
835511LV00006B/699